THE FUTURE IS NOW

Eaglemoss Ltd, 2018
1st Floor, Beaumont House,
Kensington Village, Avonmore Road,
London, W14 8TS, UK. All rights reserved.

Publisher: Maggie Calmels
Managing Editor: Ben Robinson
Design Manager: Terry Sambridge
Editor: Susie Rae
Book Design: Steve Scanlan
Introductions: James Hill

YOUR COLLECTION
DC Comics Graphic Novel Collection is published fortnightly.

DON'T MISS AN ISSUE
To make sure you receive every issue, take out a subscription
and get DC Comics Graphic Novel Collection delivered direct to
your door or place a regular order with your magazine retailer.

SUBSCRIBE and receive exclusive free gifts!
To subscribe: visit our website www.eaglemoss.com/dc-books
or post the subscription form you will find inside issue 1 to 5

UK BACK ISSUES
To order back issues:
Order online at our website www.eaglemoss.com/dc-books
or call 0371 277 0112

UK Distributor: COMAG Magazine Marketing
Call: 01895 433600

UK CUSTOMER SERVICES
Call: 0371 277 0112
Email: dc-books@eaglemoss-service.com

AUSTRALIA:
Call: (03) 9872 4000
Email: bissett@bissettmags.com.au

NEW ZEALAND:
Call: (09) 928 4493
Email: subs@

SOUTH AFRICA:
Call: (011) 265 4307
Email: service@jacklin.co.za

MALAYSIA:
Call: (03) 8020 7112
Email: sales@allscript.com

SINGAPORE:
Call: (65) 62877090
Email: sales@allscript.com

MALTA:
Call: +356 21664488
Email: info@millermalta.com

OVERSEAS BACK ISSUES
Place your order with your local magazine retailer

Visit our website: www.eaglemoss.com/dc-books

THE FUTURE
IS NOW

GEOFF JOHNS
WRITER

**IVAN REIS, JOE PRADO,
MIKE McKONE, TOM GRUMMETT**
PENCILLERS

**MARC CAMPOS, MARLO ALQUIZA
NELSON CONRAD**
INKERS

ROB LEIGH, COMICRAFT
LETTERERS

SNO-CONE STUDIOS, JEROMY COX
COLOURISTS

THE NEW TEENS TITANS CO-CREATED B
MARV WOLFMAN & GEORGE PEREZ

THE BRAVE AND THE BOLD #60
BOB HANEY
WRITER

BRUNO PREMIANI
ARTIST

Jeanine Schaefer, Eddie Berganza,
Stephen Wacker, Tom Palmer, Jr.
Editors, Original Series
George Kashdan
Editor, *The Brave and the Bold* #60

INTRODUCING...
THE FUTURE

When relaunching *Teen Titans* in 2003, writer Geoff Johns took a back-to-basics approach to the title. The book had been hugely popular for DC in the 1980s, with *The New Teen Titans* riding high in the sales charts and leading a creative renaissance at the publisher. However, subsequent versions had failed to catch on in quite the same way. In retrospect, Johns' solution to this problem was elegantly simple — he focused wholeheartedly on the generational themes at the very heart of the concept.

T Johns selected the likes of Robin III, Wonder Girl and the new Superboy to headline his cast, matching this latest generation of DC super heroes with veterans such as Cyborg and Starfire. The older Titans acted as teachers, guiding the youngsters as they struggled to find their place in a confusing and contradictory world.

T *Teen Titans: The Future is Now*, which collected stories from the title's second year, continued this approach. The Teen Titans came face-to-face with future versions of themselves — and were forced to consider the ethical choices they would make as they grew older. Similarly, in the "Lights Out" storyline, the teenagers were confronted by harsh truths that would undermine the faith they'd placed in their adult mentors.

T In Johns' hands, *Teen Titans* was all about growth and the forging of one's own identity. It pitted the natural optimism of youth against the often-stark realities of the adult world. As such, the book explored the emotional journey taken by every teenager, not just those with super-powers.

IS NOW

GEOFF JOHNS began his comics career writing STARS AND S.T.R.I.P.E. and creating Stargirl for DC Comics. He is the author of the *New York Times* best-selling graphic novels BATMAN: EARTH ONE, GREEN LANTERN: SINESTRO CORPS WAR, JUSTICE SOCIETY OF AMERICA: THY KINGDOM COME and BLACKEST NIGHT. A graduate of Michigan State University, where he studied media arts, screenwriting, film production and film theory, Johns has served as DC Entertainment's Chief Creative Officer since 2010.

BIOGRAPHIES

MIKE McKONE was pegged as an industry superstar when he first burst onto the comic book scene, illustrating JUSTICE LEAGUE INTERNATIONAL for DC Comics and *Punisher: War Zone* for Marvel Comics. In 2003, McKone teamed with writer Geoff Johns for a hugely popular relaunch of the TEEN TITANS. He followed that success with another extended run, this time headlining Marvel's *Fantastic Four* in collaboration with writer J. Michael Straczynski.

TOM GRUMMETT has been a mainstay of the comic book industry since the late 1980s. His many credits for DC Comics include SUPERMAN, SUPERBOY, ROBIN and TEEN TITANS. His action-packed pencils have also enlivened the pages of Marvel's *Avengers/Thunderbolts*, *New Thunderbolts* and *Spider-Man*.

IVAN REIS was born in 1976 in São Bernardo do Campo, São Paulo, Brazil. He started his US career in the '90s, on *Ghost* and *The Mask* for Dark Horse. In 2005, Reis began a long association with DC Comics. He has collaborated with Geoff Johns on numerous titles, including BLACKEST NIGHT,

THE STORY SO FAR...

Robin, the Boy Wonder, founded the original Teen Titans, inviting other kid sidekicks to join him in an informal organisation were they could be free from the shadow of their sometimes overbearing adult partners. The original team eventually disbanded, but was revived sometime later as the New Teen Titans.

As the individual Teen Titans grew older, many drifted away from the group. Kid Flash (Wally West) inherited the Flash identity upon Barry Allen's death and Robin (Dick Grayson) graduated to the role of Nightwing. As novice heroes emerged on the scene, Cyborg, Starfire and Beast Boy returned to the fold to tutor the next generation of Teen Titans:

RAVEN: The empathic daughter of a demon, reincarnated into the body of a teenager.

ROBIN: Tim Drake, the third youth to serve as the Dark Knight's squire.

SUPERBOY: A clone hybrid created from the DNA of Lex Luthor and Superman.

KID FLASH: Bart Allen, speedster grandson of the legendary Silver Age Flash.

WONDER GIRL: Cassie Sandsmark, granted powers by the Olympian god Zeus.

Throughout many iterations, the Teen Titans routinely encountered the bumbling villainy of Doctor Light. Even his fellow super-villains considered the hapless crook something of a buffoon. Unbeknownst to the Titans, however, Doctor Light had not always been such a lightweight. Early in his career, he had assaulted Sue Dibny, the wife of Elongated Man. To curtail Doctor Light's aberrant behaviour, the Justice League voted to have the sorceress Zatanna perform a mindwipe on him. In the process, they accidentally gave Doctor Light a partial lobotomy. Upon finally regaining his faculties, the villain vowed vengeance on the Justice League and

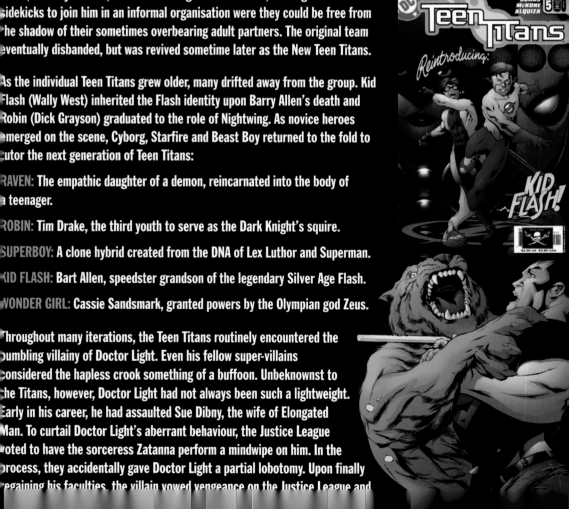

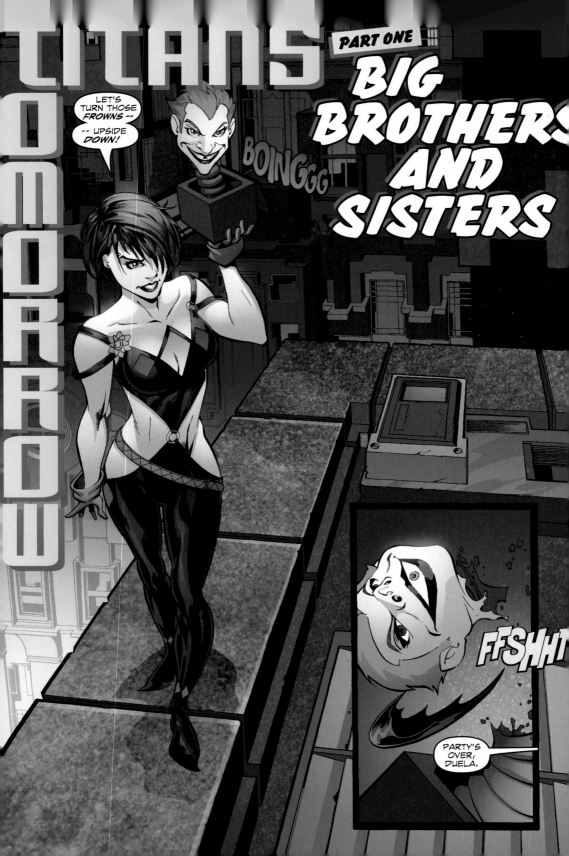

TIM.

GO AHEAD, CONNER.

WE'VE TAKEN CARE OF THE *LAST* OF H.I.V.E.'S CAMPS IN *NOTHERN SPAIN*. WE'RE HEADING BACK TO *TITANS TOWER* NOW, BUT --

-- I JUST *HEARD* THE ALARM SIGNAL. SOMEONE'S ON THE ISLAND.

SECURITY SHOULD TAKE CARE OF THEM.

IT'S *NOT*. THE SYSTEMS HAVE GONE INTO EMERGENCY SHUTDOWN.

IT *WHAT*? IT ONLY *DOES* THAT FOR *US*. IT'S PROGRAMMED TO RESPOND TO OUR --

D.N.A. I KNOW. SOMEONE MUST'VE GOT AROUND IT.

NO ONE'S BROKEN *INTO* THE TOWER. NOT SINCE KAREN AND MAL...

HEY! DON'T MOVE -- !

YOU DON'T THINK --

WE'RE AT *WAR*, AREN'T WE?

CHAKFF

BLAMM BLAMM

DARK RAVEN'S STILL ON HER PILGRIMAGE IN *ZANDIA*. WE'RE GOING TO GET HER, THEN WE'LL MEET YOU THERE.

HAVE BART PICK ME UP AT THE CAVE. I WANT US GOING IN *TOGETHER*.

ROGER THAT.

SUPERMAN OUT.

TITANS TOWER, SAN FRANCISCO.

SOMETHING'S NOT RIGHT.

I FEEL IT TOO, KORY. THE AIR SMELLS *WEIRD*.

WE MIGHT ALL BE *DIZZY* FROM THE TIME TRAVELING, CASS. HEADING BACK AND FORTH BETWEEN *CENTURIES*...

IT NEVER BOTHERS *ME*.

YEAH, BUT YOU'RE A *FLASH*. YOU GUYS ARE *SUPPOSED* TO DO THAT KIND OF STUFF.

I THINK STARFIRE'S *RIGHT*. WE'RE *NOT* HOME. NOT *YET*.

HOW DO YOU KNOW, VIC?

BESIDES THE FACT THAT ALL THE *DAMAGE* THE PERSUADER DID TO THE TOWER IS *GONE?* TAKE A *LOOK* OVER THERE.

HALL OF MENTORS

X'HAL.

THE *HALL* OF *MENTORS?* I DON'T REMEMBER...

MAX MERCURY.

MAX --?

HE WATCHED OVER ME BEFORE JAY GARRICK. MAX TAUGHT ME EVERYTHING *BOOKS* DIDN'T. EVERYTHING BOOKS *COULDN'T.*

HE DISAPPEARED INTO THE *SPEED FORCE* A WHILE AGO.

UH... WHAT'S *THIS* DOING HERE?

ARES? THE *GOD* OF WAR?

DON'T LOOK AT *ME,* CONNER.

WE HAVE SOME KIND OF *CONNECTION,* OR HE *WANTS* TO HAVE ONE. BUT I WOULD NEVER PUT HIM IN THE *MENTOR* CATEGORY.

NO WAY.

I DON'T LIKE THIS.

YOU PROBABLY WON'T LIKE *THAT* EITHER, SUPERBOY.

FWUUUMMM

STARFIRE'S *LIGHT*. HER LIGHT WILL FEEL SO... *WARM*.

DO NOT *TOUCH* HER... *WHATEVER* YOU ARE.

AAAIIIII!

NO.

DON'T YOU *SEE*?

WE'RE JUST HURTING *OURSELVES*.

STOP.

THE FLASH IS *RIGHT*, BATMAN.

MY TELEPATHY IS GETTING *CONFUSED*. YOUR BRAINWAVE FREQUENCY IS *IDENTICAL*.

SO YOU'RE SAYING --

I'M SAYING...

...TIM DRAKE...

...MEET *TIM DRAKE*.

THERE AREN'T ANY **COMPUTERS** ANYWHERE. I DON'T.

WHAT DO YOU THINK IT'S **LIKE** OUT THERE?

C'MON, TIM. THIS IS... THIS IS **BEYOND** BIZARRE. WE'RE IN THE **FUTURE**. AND **NOT** LIKE A THOUSAND YEARS FROM NOW SCIENCE FICTION-Y FUTURE.

THIS IS **OUR** FUTURE.

WHO'S TO SAY **WE'RE** FROM THE **PRESENT**? THE LEGION KEPT CALLING ME A **PRIMITIVE**.

THE **FUTURE** IS FLUID. THIS ISN'T...WHAT'S GOING TO HAPPEN.

SHOCKER.

KEEP IT UP AND YOU'RE GOING TO MAKE EVEN **MY** BRAIN **HURT.**

HELL, **THIS** MIGHT BE THE **PRESENT.**

ALL RIGHT, BUT YOU **HAVE** TO ADMIT THAT BATMAN... WELL, **YOU**...

YOU ARE **TOTALLY** HARDCORE.

DO YOU SEE HOW EVERYONE **ACTS** AROUND **BATMAN?**

...ROBIN?

I'LL **NEVER** BE BATMAN.

WHERE ARE YOU GOING?

I NEED TO GO SPEAK TO *ME*. I MEAN, *SUPERMAN*.

I CAN ASK HIM... I CAN FINALLY *TALK* TO SOMEONE ABOUT THIS WHOLE *LEX LUTHOR* STUFF. I CAN SEE IF HAVING HIS D.N.A. INSIDE ME IS GOING TO *SCREW* ME UP.

I CAN PREPARE MYSELF --

YOU SHOULDN'T DO THAT.

WHY? WHERE'S THE *RULE BOOK* ON *TIME TRAVEL*?

LOOK, TIM. I'M JUST GOING TO ASK IF IT'S EVER A *PROBLEM*.

YOU *SAW* THAT STATUE.

IT'S *NOT* A GOOD IDEA.

OPINION NOTED, RIGHT. BUT I *HAVE* TO DO THIS.

I'LL BE BACK IN, LIKE, *FIVE* MINUTES.

BATMAN...

WHAT EVER *MAKE* ME WANT TO BE *BATMAN*?

SPEEDY? THAT'S NOT CISSIE. WHO -- ?

SPEEDY

WE SHOULDN'T LET THEM STAY HERE.

WHERE ELSE WOULD WE PUT THEM, CONNER? THE PHANTOM ZONE? YOU *KNOW* WHAT HAPPENED WHEN WE IMPRISONED *BROTHER BLOOD* AND *BRAINIAC.*

I'M JUST SAYING, CASSIE, I *KNOW* WHAT I WAS *LIKE.* EACH *ONE* OF US KNOWS WHAT WE WERE LIKE.

WE WERE *KIDS,* CONNER.

TODAY, WE'RE *BETTER.*

WE'LL HANDLE THIS *MY* WAY. IT WON'T HURT THEM, BUT IT *WILL* GET THE JOB DONE.

I STILL CAN'T BELIEVE THIS IS HAPPENING.

BELIEVE IT, LORENA.

RRFF... AND WHAT ABOUT *HIM?*

HE'LL *TALK,* GAR.

HE'LL TELL US WHAT VICTOR AND THE OTHERS ARE UP TO --

ROBIN!

TIM, WE'VE GOT TO GET OUT OF HERE.

YOU LOOK LIKE **HELL.**

I **KNOW.**

I **TOLD** YOU, CONNER --

-- ASKING YOUR **FUTURE SELF** WHAT YOU SHOULD **"WATCH OUT"** FOR, KNOWING THINGS ABOUT **TOMORROW,** IT'S **NEVER** A GOOD THING.

THIS IS **DIFFERENT.**

I WENT DOWN THERE, I WENT DOWN TO TALK TO THIS **SUPERMAN,** TO **ME,** AND I SAW...

I JUST SAW THE **TITANS,** I MEAN **US...**

SUPERMAN... HE BURNED DEATHSTROKE'S **ARM** OFF.

WHAT?

I'M TELLING YOU. IN THE **FUTURE...**

WE'RE **PSYCHOS!** WE'RE JERKS!

WE'RE FREAKIN' **BAD GUYS!**

RRRRFF

LORENA -- ?

HIS *MIND* IS STILL RESISTING MY TELEPATHY. I CAN *PUSH* IT FURTHER, BUT YOU KNOW WHAT HAPPENED TO TEMPEST.

TEMPEST WAS A *TRAITOR.*

SORRY I'M LATE. WHAT'S -- ?

WHERE *WERE* YOU?

THE...*SPEED FORCE.* VISITING WITH MAX.

COME ON. LET ME *FINISH* THIS, TIM.

WE STILL HAVE BORDER PATROL IN KANSAS. AND *HAWK* AND *DOVE* HAVE BEEN SPOTTED OUTSIDE SMALLVILLE AGAIN, NO DOUBT TRYING TO FREE *MIA* FROM THE *FORTRESS* OF *PARADISE.*

PA MIGHT BE IN TROUBLE.

CONNER IS *RIGHT.* WE HAVE *IMPORTANT* WORK TO DO.

AND IT STARTS WITH THE *CHILDREN* UPSTAIRS.

WHEN RAVEN'S SOUL-SELVES INTEGRATED, ROBIN WAS THROWN *CLEAR.*

WE NEED TO GO BACK. WE NEED TO GO BACK AND GET TIM. YOU SAW WHAT THEY DID TO DEATHSTROKE--

I... I CAN'T TELEPORT, CONNER. I NEED TO... REST. JUST GIVE ME A MINUTE TO...

LET HER REST. THEY *CAN'T* HURT ROBIN WITHOUT HURTING *BATMAN.* WE GET THE TIME MACHINE THEN WE HEAD BACK TO THE TOWER--

I'LL GO BY *MYSELF* IF I HAVE --

WE DON'T STAND A CHANCE UNLESS WE DO THIS TOGETHER.

VIC--

CONNER.

CYBORG'S RIGHT.

WE HAVE TO DO THIS *TOGETHER.*

AN ALARM?

WEEEEOOOP WEEEEOOOP

FLA[SH]
THE COSMIC T[READMILL]

MY BAD I THINK.

WEEEEOOOP

WEEEEOOOP WEEEEOOOP

SO NO TIME MACHINE. WHAT NOW?

WEEEEOOOP

BACK TO THE TOWER? TO GET ROBIN?

FIRST WE VACATE. NO TELLING WHO THIS BUZZING'S GOING TO BRING--

HELLO, VICTOR.

MAN, I LOOK YOUNG.

WHO--?

CALM YOUR CIRCUITS, PAL.

NEW YORK CITY.

...TEN YEARS FROM NOW.

ANOTHER BEAUTIFUL DAY, ISN'T IT?

GO AHEAD, PAL. PEDESTRIANS FIRST!

THANKS, BUDDY!

-- IN FLORIDA YESTERDAY, WHERE CYBORG AND THE TITANS EAST HALTED A HURRICANE CREATED BY MR. TWISTER THAT THREATENED TO ENGULF MOST OF THE STATE.

EASTERN PRESIDENT DUNCAN PRAISED THE HEROES FOR THEIR EFFORTS.

MEANWHILE, CONFLICT ALONG THE BORDER CONTINUED THIS MORNING WHEN FREEDOM FIGHTERS RED STAR AND MIRAGE WERE ARRESTED OUTSIDE OF KANSAS CITY AND CHARGED WITH TREASON AGAINST THE WEST.

THE WESTERNERS. IT'S A SHAME.

JUST THANK YOUR STARS YOU WERE BORN IN MARYLAND, MARGARET.

WHOA! NO WAY!

IT'S *THEM*, IT'S *THEM*!

NO OFFENSE, "VIC," BUT WHY SHOULD WE TRUST *YOU* GUYS?

AM I THE ONLY ONE THAT NOTICED *RAVAGER* IS ON THEIR SIDE?

IT'S COMPLICATED, BUT IF YOU WANT TO FIND *ROBIN* AND GET BACK --

AND YOU AND *ME* ARE SUPPOSED TO BE *BEST FRIENDS.* SO WHY IS *MY* FUTURE SELF STUCK ON THE WEST COAST WITH THOSE PSYCHOS?

BECAUSE YOU *REFUSED* TO HAVE ANYTHING TO DO WITH ME --

NO DETAILS ON THE PAST, TERRA. *CYBORG'S* BEEN THROUGH THIS *DOZENS* OF TIMES.

I'VE BEEN THROUGH *WHAT*, BUMBLEBEE?

I'VE BEEN PREPARING THIS TEAM FOR YOUR ARRIVAL FOR THE LAST THREE YEARS. EVER SINCE THE TITANS WEST FORCED THIS COUNTRY TO *SPLIT* IN *HALF.*

THEY WANTED TO RUN A MILITANT STATE, ONE *FREE* OF *CRIME, POVERTY* AND *DISEASE.* FOR THE MOST PART, THEY ACTUALLY SUCCEEDED.

BUT THE PEOPLE GAVE UP THEIR *FREEDOM* FOR IT. THERE WERE REBELLIONS ALL ALONG THE *WEST COAST* THAT BATMAN HAD DARK RAVEN STOP.

THE *WICKED WITCH* OF THE *WEST* ATE UP THEIR *FREE WILL* AND *HOPE.*

VIC AND I GATHERED TOGETHER OUR *OWN* TITANS. WE'VE MANAGED TO FREE *TWELVE* OF THE *FIFTY* STATES.

WE'RE TRYING TO FREE *KANSAS.*

BUT *HOW* DID WE TURN OUT THAT WAY? WHY ARE *WE* SUCH LUNATICS?

YEAH. IT'S LIKE IT'D BE BETTER IF THE TITANS JUST *BROKE* UP WHEN WE GET BACK HOME.

I...I WOULD NEVER DEPRIVE PEOPLE OF THEIR FREE WILL.

AND I DON'T WANT TO TURN INTO THAT *ANIMAL MAN,* VIC. MAYBE BART IS RIGHT. MAYBE WE HAVE TO BREAK UP TO *STOP* THIS.

THAT'S NOT WHAT I MEANT.

NO. YOU...YOU *CAN'T* BREAK APART.

THAT'S WHAT *MAKES* THIS ALL *HAPPEN.*

WHAT? MAKES *WHAT* HAPPEN?

IN *OUR* TIMELINE, THE TEEN TITANS WERE THROWN TEN YEARS IN THE FUTURE. THEY FACED THEMSELVES. AND WHEN THEY RETURNED --

-- THE TEAM *SPLIT.* EVERYONE WENT THEIR OWN WAY.

THE TITANS WEREN'T THERE TO HELP SAVE THE HEROES DURING THE CRISIS, SUPERBOY...

THE TITANS RE-FORMED FOUR YEARS AGO. BUT THE TIME THEY SPENT APART ERASED WHO THEY USED TO BE. THEY WERE INFLUENCED BY *OUTSIDE* FORCES.

SO IN ORDER TO PREVENT THIS FUTURE...

THE TITANS NEED TO STAY *TOGETHER.*

STARFIRE? ARE YOU -- ?

EVERYONE IS HERE. EVERYONE HAS A *LIFE.* EXCEPT *ME.*

YOU *HAVE* A FUTURE, KORY. AND IT'S A *WONDERFUL* ONE.

WHERE -- ?

FAR AWAY FROM ALL OF *THIS.* WITH NIGHTWING.

WHEN YOU GET BACK, YOU *NEED* TO SEEK HIM OUT. YOU NEED TO BE THERE FOR HIM.

DON'T FORGET THAT.

WHO ARE *YOU?*

BOOOMM

FLASH?!

HE'S ONE OF *THEM!* GET --

WAIT. THE *FLASH* ISN'T YOUR *ENEMY.*

BART'S BEEN WORKING WITH *US.* HE'S --

YOUR FATHER TOLD YOU WHERE THE... COSMIC TREADMILL IS...RIGHT?

HE GAVE ME THE SCHEMATICS OF THE CAVE WHEN I PICKED HIM UP FROM THE WEST TOWER. THAT WAS *NICE* OF HIM.

THE BATCAVE.

HE DID IT FOR THE *MONEY,* MARVEL. HE DIDN'T DO IT FOR *ME.*

BUT *I DID,* ROSE.

THEY *KNOW.* THEY KNOW I'VE BEEN...WORKING WITH YOU.

AND THEY'RE... COMING --

KRRRSSS4HTTT

HEAT VISION...

GIVE US THE *KIDS* AND WE LET *YOUR* TITANS *LIVE,* VICTOR.

YOU KNOW WHAT I'M GONNA SAY, DON'T YOU, VIC?

YEP.

HELL, NO.

TITANS TOWER.

SAN FRANCISCO.

SATURDAY, 4:45 P.M.

HEY, MAN.

HEY.

CAN I BORROW A SHIRT? I DON'T HAVE ANYTHING HERE WITHOUT AN "S" ON IT.

BART IS MAKING US GO TO DAVE AND BUSTERS. PLAY SOME GAMES. HAVE SOME FUN.

SOMETIMES I THINK WE *FORGOT* HOW TO DO THAT.

IF WHAT WE JUST SAW TAUGHT US *ANYTHING*, TIM--

-- IT'S THAT WE NEED TO *LIGHTEN* UP.

AND WE NEED TO STICK *TOGETHER*.

NO MATTER *WHAT*.

NO MATTER *WHAT*, CONNER.

EPILOGUE.

SMALLVILLE.

...TEN YEARS FROM NOW.

I NEED SOME ADVICE, PA.

THE *TEEN TITANS* ESCAPED. BACK TO THE *PAST.*

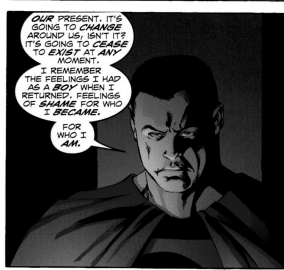

OUR PRESENT. IT'S GOING TO *CHANGE* AROUND US, ISN'T IT? IT'S GOING TO *CEASE* TO *EXIST* AT *ANY* MOMENT.

I REMEMBER THE FEELINGS I HAD AS A *BOY* WHEN I RETURNED. FEELINGS OF *SHAME* FOR WHO I *BECAME.*

FOR WHO I *AM.*

WHO YOU *ARE,* KON-EL?

YOU ARE MY *SON.*

AND THE *WORLD* SHOULD FEEL SHAME FOR TURNING THEIR BACKS ON *YOU.* JUST AS THEY DID *ME.*

DO NOT *FEAR* YOUR FUTURE.

EMBRACE IT. JUST AS YOU EMBRACE CASSANDRA.

I EXPECT A *GRANDCHILD* FROM YOU TWO ONE OF THESE DAYS.

I WON'T LET YOU DOWN, PA.

YOU NEVER *DID*, SON. YOU NEVER DID.

I REMEMBER --

AAAHH!

-- WHAT YOU DID TO ME.

HNN.

YOU WEREN'T EXACTLY... AN *INNOCENT*, LIGHT.

NO, I SUPPOSE *NOT*.

BUT I HAD A *TASTE* FOR INNOCENCE.

YOUR *DAUGHTER* IS GOING TO *DIE*.

I DON'T *HAVE* A DAUGHTER, YOU IDIOT.

BUT YOU HAVE... *SPEEDY*.

YOU DON'T REALLY BELIEVE I PICKED *TODAY* OUT OF A *HAT*, DO YOU?

I PAID THE CALCULATOR GOOD MONEY TO FIND OUT WHEN YOUR PROTÉGÉ WAS JOINING THE *TITANS*.

AND THAT'S *TODAY*.

LEAVE THE KIDS *OUT* OF THIS.

THE *JUSTICE LEAGUE* TOOK MY *MIND* AND *FED* ME TO THEIR *YOUNG*.

THEY MADE ME A *PLAYTHING* TO BUILD THEIR *CHILDREN'S* SELF-CONFIDENCE.

DON'T YOU UNDERSTAND, GREEN ARROW?

YOU AND THE OTHERS -- *YOU* PUT THEM *IN* THIS.

YOU PUT THEM *RIGHT* IN THE *MIDDLE*.

OLLIE TOLD ME HE HAD **ONE** THING ON HIS MIND WHEN HE JOINED THE LEAGUE.

HE SAID, "THAT **FIRST** TIME YOU'RE UP TO BAT, WHATEVER YA DO --

-- **DON'T MISS** THE **TARGET.**"

I HAVEN'T REALLY GONE TO HIGH SCHOOL. NEVER HUNG AROUND PEOPLE MY OWN AGE.

BUT THE TITANS SEEM PRETTY COOL.

D.N.A. SCAN COMPLETE. **MIA DEARDEN,** YOU HAVE BEEN CLEARED FOR ACCESS TO TITANS TOWER.

FSSH

AND I WANT TO MAKE NEW FRIENDS.

...ACTUALLY, WAIT. **NO I DON'T!**

THAT'S **OLLIE** TALKING!

PLEASE STEP IN AND BUCKLE UP. THANK YOU.

I'M GONNA KEEP HEARING HIS LITTLE, SCRATCHY VOICE IN THE BACK OF MY HEAD -- **BARKING** AT ME?

AT LEAST WHEN HE'S **AROUND** I CAN TELL HIM TO SHUT UP.

MAYBE THIS IS A **MISTAKE.**

UH, HEY. IT'S MIA DEARDEN. I'M CLEARED OR WHATEVER. CAN WE GO BACK?

DAMMIT.

GOTTA PRETEND YOU'RE LIKE THEM THEN. JUST A KID THINKING ABOUT BOYS, MUSIC AND WHICH COLLEGE YOU'RE GOING TO GO TO.

ISN'T THAT WHAT **OTHER** TEENAGERS WORRY ABOUT?

I MEAN, WHAT'S A NORMAL DAY LIKE FOR THE TITANS?

KID FLASH IS OLLIE'S FAVORITE OF THESE NEW KIDS. SAID HE REMINDS HIM OF BARRY, BUT WITHOUT THE CONSERVATIVE ATTITUDE.

KRRRZZT!

ELECTRICAL BIO-DISCHARGE. KID FLASH IS GONNA BE OUT FOR A SEC.

WHAT DO YOU THINK, WONDER GIRL? CAN YOU *FLY* FASTER THAN *SOUND*?

I DON'T NEED TO.

I THOUGHT MAYBE, SOMETHING *WEIRD* WENT DOWN.

LIKE...JERICHO WAS BACK! JUMPING INTO PEOPLE'S BODIES OR WHATEVER.

JERICHO?

TITAN WITH AN *AFRO.*

I'VE SPENT ALL *WEEK* READING UP ON YOU GUYS. I EVEN KNOW WHO FLAMEBIRD AND MIRAGE ARE.

WHO?

PRETTY BOY. NOT MUCH BEHIND THOSE BLUE EYES THOUGH, IS THERE?

I DIDN'T... IS MR. STONE GONNA BE ALL RIGHT?

'COURSE HE IS.

WE'RE TALKING ABOUT *CYBORG.*

WHO IS THE *ONLY* TITAN I CAN'T GET A READ ON. HE'S IN HIS 20'S, HE'S *BEEN* A TITAN.

DON'T WORRY, MIA. HIS SYSTEM IS ALREADY COMING BACK ON-LINE.

VRREEEP

AND THERE'S NO *PERMANENT* DAMAGE TO HIS ORGANICS.

RAVEN STARES AT ME...IT MAKES ME WANT TO PUT MY HOOD BACK UP --

-- AND BURY MY *FACE* IN THE SAND. IS IT *MY* PROBLEM... OR IS IT *HERS?*

WHAT HIT ME?

UM... SORRY?

YEAH, OLLIE.

RIGHT ON TARGET.

THIS IS GONNA BE A *LONG* WEEKEND.

SORRY.

YOU CAN *STOP* APOLOGIZING, MIA.

I SHORT-CIRCUITED MY LEADER AND MADE MYSELF LOOK LIKE A *JERK* IN FRONT OF THE TITANS.

SORRY SORRY SORRY.

MY NERVOUS SYSTEM IS ALMOST FINISHED REBOOTING, FEELING'S BACK IN MY ARMS. AND YOU *DIDN'T* LOOK LIKE A *JERK*.

I JUST DON'T WANT TO BE THE, Y'KNOW, *"ANNOYING"* MEMBER. I KNOW WHAT THE LEAGUE THINKS OF GREEN ARROW. HE'S LOUD, HE'S OPINIONATED --

YOU'LL BE FINE.

BEING A YOUNG HERO, TRYING TO FIND YOUR PLACE IN THE WORLD. IT'S HARD.

ESPECIALLY WHEN YOU GOT GUYS LIKE *GREEN ARROW* AND *SUPERMAN* WATCHING YOUR EVERY MOVE.

"BUT THAT'S WHY *NIGHTWING* FOUNDED THE *TEEN TITANS* BACK WHEN HE WAS *ROBIN*. ALONG WITH ARSENAL WHEN *HE* WAS SPEEDY; THE FIRST KID FLASH, THE ORIGINAL WONDER GIRL AND AQUALAD.

"THEY MADE THE TEAM A PLACE THEY COULD BE THEMSELVES, INSTEAD OF HAVING TO STAND UP *STRAIGHT* AND WATCH *EVERY* WORD THEY SAID."

YEARS LATER, *RAVEN* HELPED GET THE TEAM BACK TOGETHER TO FIGHT HER FATHER, *TRIGON*. BROUGHT NEW MEMBERS IN LIKE *ME*, KORY AND GAR.

IT WAS AN AMAZING TIME.

"BUT NOW, IT'S A *NEW* GENERATION'S TEAM. A *NEW* TEEN TITANS.

"AND YOU'RE WELCOME TO BE A PART OF IT, MIA."

YEAH... YEAH, WE'LL SEE.

POOL'S DOWN THERE. IT'S HEATED, BUT WATCH OUT IF BEAST BOY USES IT BEFORE YOU.

GAR DOES LAPS AS A *PENGUIN*, KEEPS THE TEMP AT FIFTY DEGREES.

YOUR LOCKER'S --

YEP.

TAKE IT THE *ARROW* MEANS THAT'S *MINE*.

WHO WON ALL THE TROPHIES?

I DID.

YOU...?

BEFORE THE *ACCIDENT*. I WAS A REAL COMPETITOR.

I *LOVED* EVERYTHING ABOUT SPORTS.

HHN. AND I WAS *GOOD*.

YOU MISS IT?

EVERY DAY.

BUT IF THINGS WERE DIFFERENT, I'D MISS BEING A *TITAN* MORE.

THERE'S A... THERE'S A *LOT* OF LOCKERS.

THERE'S A *LOT* OF TITANS OUT IN THE *WORLD*.

YOU JUST HAVEN'T MET THEM ALL YET.

HERE WE GO.

"STAYING FAT FOR SARAH BYRNES"? "SPEAK"? THESE ARE...THESE ARE ALL MY *FAVORITE* BOOKS.

WE HAVE A LIBRARY ON THE FOURTH FLOOR, ACROSS FROM ROBIN'S FORENSICS LAB.

GREEN ARROW SAID YOU LIKED TO READ.

COOL.

HE TOLD ME ALL ABOUT YOU, MIA.

NG TIDE

SPEAK

STAYING FAT FOR SARAH BYRNES

NOT COOL.

RAN AWAY FROM AN ABUSIVE HOME WHEN YOU WERE PRETTY YOUNG. SPENT SOME TIME ON THE STREETS, SURVIVING ANY WAY YOU COULD.

UNTIL *ROBIN HOOD* SHOWED UP AND OFFERED YOU A PLACE IN HIS BAND OF MERRY MEN. TURNS OUT YOU'RE A *NATURAL* WITH A BOW AND ARROW.

THAT BASICALLY IT?

BASICALLY...

I'M NOTHING LIKE THESE OTHER KIDS, AM I?

YOU'RE NOT A *CLONE*, YOU'RE NOT FROM THE *FUTURE*, YOU'RE NOT *HALF-MAN HALF-MACHINE.*

YOU'RE JUST A GIRL WITH A TALENT.

AND, FROM WHAT I'VE BEEN TOLD, A HERO'S INSTINCT.

EVEN *IF* YOU COVERED ME IN *ICE.*

I FINALLY FIGURED OUT WHO CYBORG IS.

THE *TIN MAN* WITH A *HEART.*

I GOT SOMETHIN' FOR YOU.

WHAT ARE--?

THEY BELONGED TO SPEEDY BEFORE HE TRADED IN THE *TRICK ARROWS* FOR HIS *ARSENAL* IDENTITY.

ROY WANTED YOU TO HAVE THEM. SAID HE MISSED YOUR SEVENTEENTH BIRTHDAY.

IT WAS, UH, LAST WEEK.

HE MENTIONED THE MAGNESIUM FLARES WERE PROBABLY EXPIRED. WHICHEVER ONES THOSE ARE.

THESE. WITH THE GLASS BULBS ON THE END.

HEY.

WHAT'S THE *BLUE* ONE FOR?

DON'T KNOW.

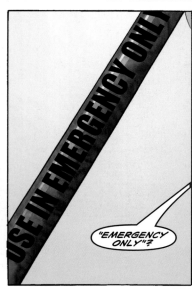

USE IN EMERGENCY ONLY

"EMERGENCY ONLY"?

CYBORG. I ALSO... I NEED TO TELL YOU ALL SOMETHING ELSE--

YO!

AAAA!

SORRY, SPEEDY, BUT... YOU GUYS BETTER *SEE* THIS.

--MIKE DAVIS REPORTING LIVE JUST OUTSIDE OF THE FRANKLIN INSTITUTE. WE'RE STILL UNSURE OF EXACTLY **HOW** MANY ARE INJURED JUST YET, BUT **DOZENS** ARE SUFFERING FROM THIRD DEGREE BURNS, OTHERS **BLINDED.**

ONE SECURITY GUARD REPORTED DEAD.

WHAT IS IT? WHAT'S GOING ON?

THE LAST TIME DOCTOR LIGHT WAS SEEN HERE WAS SEVERAL MONTHS AGO...WHERE HE WAS ARRESTED BY THE **RAY** FOR SHOPLIFTING FROM THE FIRST FOOD MARKET THREE BLOCKS AWAY.

JUST A FEW WEEKS BACK, DR. LIGHT WAS INVOLVED IN AN ATTACK ON THE JUSTICE LEAGUE.

BUT IT WAS THIRTY MINUTES AGO THAT **EVERY** NEWS STATION IN THE CITY WAS CONTACTED BY DOCTOR LIGHT WHEN HE TOOK **CONTROL** OF THE MUSEUM.

HE WANTED EVERY **REPORTER** AND **CAMERA** IN THE CITY HERE. WHY? WE'RE NOT...

WAIT. WAIT, THERE'S A **LIGHT.** A BRIGHT...IT'S HOT... INTENSE.

IT'S...

GREEN ARROW IS MINE.

OH, MY GOD!

OLLIE!

I WANT MY REPUTATION BACK. I WANT THE TEEN TITANS. AND ONLY THEM.

IF ANYONE ELSE OUTSIDE THE TITANS SHOWS, GREEN ARROW DIES. COME. FACE ME. NOW.

OLLIE...

FFSSSHHHH

NO!

WHAT DO WE DO?!

WE RUN OVER TO PHILADELPHIA, RIGHT?

AND WE PUT *LIGHT* OUT.

HOW'D AN *IDIOT* LIKE LIGHT AMBUSH GREEN ARROW?

VEET

VIC! THE OUTSIDERS JUST SAW DOCTOR LIGHT'S BROADCAST.

MIA, DON'T WORRY. WE'RE ON OUR WAY--

ARSENAL?! DIDN'T YOU *HEAR* HIM? HE SAID *NO* ONE BUT THE TITANS.

SHE'S CORRECT, ROY.

I CAN'T JUST SIT HERE AND *WAIT*, RAVEN. THIS IS... THIS IS *OLLIE* WE'RE TALKING ABOUT.

AND NO MATTER *WHERE* WE ARE, WE'RE *STILL* TITANS.

VICTOR. I HAVE AN *IDEA.*

VEET

DOC LIGHT WAS THE PRIME SUSPECT IN SUE DIBNY'S MURDER, RIGHT?

YES. AND THERE'VE BEEN RUMORS THROUGHOUT THE SUPER-VILLAIN COMMUNITY--

THROUGHOUT THE "SUPER-VILLAIN COMMUNITY"? WHAT? ARE YOU SAYING THEY HANG OUT TOO?

OF COURSE, THEY DO, CONNER. JUST NOT IN BIG BUILDINGS SHAPED LIKE A "T".

SO WHAT'D YOU HEAR?

THAT DOCTOR LIGHT WASN'T ALWAYS A PATHETIC LOSER GETTING HIS BUTT HANDED TO HIM BY KIDS IN TIGHTS.

HE WAS A PSYCHOPATH, A REAL THREAT, AND THEN HE GOT MESSED UP.

"MESSED UP"? WHAT'S THAT MEAN?

HE LOST WHATEVER MADE HIM SMART, CASS.

FROM WHAT? DONNA KICKING HIM IN THE HEAD ONE TOO MANY TIMES?

YOU THINK THE RUMORS ARE TRUE?

WELL... BATMAN DIDN'T KNOW ANYTHING ABOUT IT.

HE SAID HE DIDN'T.

20TH STREET

YOU THINK HE'S INSIDE WITH GREEN ARROW?

IF WE GET CLOSER I CAN USE MY INFRARED SCANNERS.

HEY, LISTEN. IF I GET...HURT... JUST LET ME TAKE CARE OF MYSELF, ALL RIGHT?

WHAT? YOU GOT SOMETHING TO PROVE--?

HEY! WHAT'S WITH THE NEWS COPTERS?

HE SAID HE WANTED HIS REP BACK.

PFF. REP? HE NEVER HAD ONE.

YEAH. LIGHT IS JUST TRYING TO GET ATTENTION ANY WAY HE CAN. TOTAL GLORY HOUND.

KRRRKKZZTT

JUST KEEP YOUR EYES OPEN, GAR--

WELCOME, TITANS.

LIGHT?

WE'RE HERE. SHOW YOURSELF.

YEAH, YA COWARD!

NAMES USED TO BOTHER ME, SUPERBOY. WHEN MY SELF-CONFIDENCE AND EGO WERE TRANSFORMED INTO THAT OF A TEENAGED GIRL.

HEY!

THE JUSTICE LEAGUE STOLE MY DIGNITY.

THAT IS WHY I CONFRONT THE EVIL AROUND ME.

I'M NOT TALKING ABOUT *POWERS* OR *ABILITIES*. I'M TALKING ABOUT *MORALS*.

YOU LOOK UP TO *FALSE HEROES*.

I CAN BARELY SEE.

THE LENSES IN MY MASK CAUGHT MOST OF THE *FLARE*, BART. JUST STICK CLOSE.

I CAN STILL SMELL HIS CHEAP COLOGNE. MAN, IT *STINKS*.

I THINK HE CAN HEAR YOU, GAR.

OH, NO. WE MIGHT HURT HIS *FEELINGS*.

IF I HURT HIM?!

KKRRAAKKKAAA

I CAN FEEL MY SKIN *BLISTER.*

I HEAL IT.

AND PRAY.

THOUGH I KNOW MY PRAYERS HAVE *NEVER BEEN HEARD* --

-- BY ANYONE *GOOD.*

YOU BETTER WATCH YOURSELVES.

IF YOU LEARN THE *WRONG* THING, OR MAYBE IF YOU THREATEN TO *REPLACE* YOUR *MENTORS* SOONER THAN THEY *WANT* TO BE REPLACED --

-- THEY MIGHT DO IT TO *YOU* TOO.

THEY'LL TAKE YOUR *MIND.*

NO MATTER HOW *SMALL* IT MIGHT BE.

THOUGH THERE *IS* SOMETHING VALUABLE *INSIDE* YOU, SUPERBOY.

I CAN *SEE* IT ALL AROUND US, AND WEAVE IT LIKE A *SPIDER* WEAVES HIS *WEB*.

WH-WHAT...?

LIGHT.

YOUR *HEAT VISION*, SUPERBOY. LET ME *SEE* IT.

GIVE IT TO ME.

AAARRRRGG!

FWPP

-- FIGHTING SEEMS TO HAVE STOPPED FOR THE MOMENT, THE DEVASTATION NOW COVERING OVER A CITY BLOCK. THE SMOKE IS OBSCURING THE VIEW BUT WHAT WE DO KNOW IS THAT SOMEHOW...

DOCTOR LIGHT IS STILL STANDING.

OFFICIALS CONTINUE TO EXTEND THE EVACUATION ANOTHER SIX SQUARE BLOCKS, BUT WITH THE POWER STILL OUT AND NIGHT FALLING, THERE HAVE BEEN REPORTS OF RIOTING AND UNREST --

WPHL - LIVE

STARFIRE'S PLAN IS ALREADY IN MOTION.

AND DOCTOR LIGHT?

WHEN THIS IS FINISHED...

SHNNGGG

...THEY WANT HIM.

GREEN ARROW.

WAKE UP.

NNN?

FWASHHH

LIGHT...?
LEAVE HER...ALONE, YOU PIECE OF TRASH.

CLOSE YOUR MOUTH FOR ONCE --

-- AND LISTEN.

FWPP

ARR.

I'VE BEEN WONDERING WHO ELSE YOU DID THIS TO. DOCTOR POLARIS, FELIX FAUST, OR THE TATTOOED MAN?

WAS IT ONLY THE VILLAINS?

OR DID OTHER HEROES GET IN YOUR WAY TOO?

IS THIS HOW YOU *KEEP* YOUR *KIDS* IN LINE? HOW YOU GET THEM TO *OBEY* AND *BEHAVE?*

SURELY FOR *SOME* OF THEM, THAT IS THE ONLY WAY.

ESPECIALLY *YOURS. I KNOW* SOME OF YOUR *SECRETS.*

LOOK AT WHAT HAPPENED TO THE *FIRST* SPEEDY. AND *THIS* ONE. YOU HAVE REAL *LUCK* WITH SIDEKICKS. BUT DON'T WORRY --

-- I'M *CERTAIN* YOU'LL FIND A *NEW* ONE TO BRAINWASH *SOON* ENOUGH.

TAKING ON AN UNCONSCIOUS *HIGH SCHOOL GIRL.* A *SEVENTEEN-*YEAR-OLD *GIRL.* NO MATTER *WHAT* YOU DO, *LIGHT --* DEEP *DOWN --*

-- YOU'RE *STILL* JUST A *COWARD.*

VUUUAKK

I WISH YOU HADN'T MADE ME *DO* THAT.

I WANTED YOU TO *WATCH* HER *BURN --*

THERE HE IS!

THE KID NEXT TO ME IS *CAPTAIN MARVEL JUNIOR.*

HE'S OKAY, JUST A LITTLE TOO INTO THE *RETRO* THING FOR MY TASTES.

THANKS FOR THE HAND, BUT I HAD IT.

YOU HAD IT?!

LOVES ALL THAT *ROCKABILLY* CRAP. FLAME SHIRTS AND HOT DICE BELT BUCKLES.

WHATEVER, MARVEL. WHY'S EVERYONE HERE?

STARFIRE CALLED US. WE MAY NOT BE ON THE *ACTIVE* ROSTER, BUT WE'RE STILL *TITANS.*

AND THAT'S WHAT DOCTOR LIGHT WANTED, RIGHT?

ELVIS PRESLEY.

GREATEST MODERN-DAY PHILOSOPHER IF YOU ASK *ME.*

LOOKS LIKE HE NEVER HEARD THE SAYING, *"DO WHAT'S RIGHT FOR YOU AS LONG AS YOU DON'T HURT NO ONE."*

WHO THE HELL SAID *THAT?*

I PREFER *SID VICIOUS* MYSELF.

THANKS FOR THE LIFT, GENTS. SURE THE *NEWSBOYS* ABOARD THANK YOU, TOO.

WHO ARE--?

NAME'S *HAWK,* S-BOY. MY SIS IS A FRIEND OF THE *TITANS.* THOUGHT I'D HITCH ALONG.

BEST GET GOIN', HUH?

NOT SURE WHO THIS ENGLISH CHICK IS--

--BUT I LIKE HER.

I WANT A PIECE OF LIGHT'S CAPE FOR MY SCRAPBOOK!

DOCTOR LIGHT KIDNAPPED *GREEN ARROW* AND THEN HE MADE ALL THE NEWS CREWS COME TO THE CENTER OF THE CITY.

HE CHALLENGED THE TITANS AND SAID IF *ANYONE* BUT THE TITANS CAME HE'D *KILL* ARROW.

WE WERE *WAVE ONE,* I GUESS.

AQUALAD. IT'S BEEN A LONG--

--ARRR!

I'VE *FROZEN* THE WATER IN HIS EYES.

THEN I'LL *MELT* IT.

STINGERS AREN'T DOING MUCH DAMAGE, MAL.

BACK OFF AND *PLUG* YOUR EARS, BUMBLEBEE.

THE HERALD IS COMING OUT OF RETIREMENT FOR *ONE.*

LAST. SONG.

KRRRSHHHT

HOW ABOUT A *WHIFF* OF MY *FLOWER,* DOC?

AHAHAHAHA!

WHO DO YOU THINK YOU'RE *FACING,* DUELA?

YOU THINK SHEER *NUMBERS* WILL *HELP* YOU?

FSSSSSSS

DOVE, WE'RE MISSIN' THE BLEEDIN' *FUN!*

COME ON! WE...

DAWN?

SHE IS... WOUNDED.

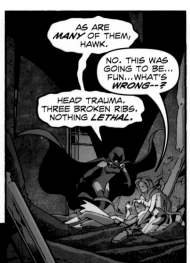

AS ARE *MANY* OF THEM, HAWK.

NO. THIS WAS GOING TO BE... FUN...WHAT'S *WRONG--?*

HEAD TRAUMA. THREE BROKEN RIBS. NOTHING *LETHAL.*

MEANING I CAN *HEAL* HER.

GIVE UP AND YOU DON'T GET *HURT,* LIGHT.

I CAN *SEE* RIGHT *THROUGH* IT.

BOOM

YOU THINK YOUR *ILLUSION-WEAVING* FOOLS *ME,* MIRAGE?

SEE THROUGH *THIS.*

KRRSHHT

FRRZZZZZ

DOSTAL.

RED STAR.

MY COMRADE.

THOOM

AWAY FROM THEM, BOLVAN.

THOOM

THOOM

BWWWOOSSH

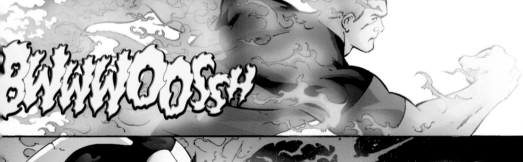

KRRK

'MEMBER WHAT I SAID, WILDEBEEST!

IT'S *OKAY* TO DRAW BLOOD *THIS* TIME.

GRRRRFF!

IS IT GETTING *DARKER?*

HE'S *POWERING* UP. HE'S *SUCKING* IN ALL THE *AMBIENT* LIGHT.

TITANS! GET--

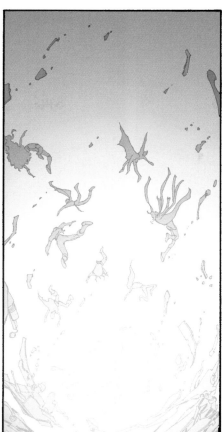

COME **ON**, OLLIE... ≶**UGGF**.≶

MAN, YOU GOTTA LAY OFF THOSE CHILI DOGS.

"HE THAT LIVES UPON **HOPE** WILL DIE FASTING."

BENJAMIN FRANKLIN. THE **FATHER** OF MODERN-DAY **LIGHT**. A **HERO** FROM MY CHILDHOOD.

I HAD THE CHANCE TO BE A **HERO**. MY MIND WAS BRILLIANT. MY...**NEEDS** UNFORTUNATELY GOT IN THE **WAY**.

HELL.

ALONG WITH **YOU**. BUT I'VE **ACCEPTED** MY **DESTINY**.

TO SPILL YOUNG BLOOD.

OKAY, **MYSTERY** ARROW. HERE GOES NOTH--

SPEEDY!

GIVE UP NOW.

YOUR *KIDNEYS* WOULD'VE BEEN HERE.

TELL ME, STONE.

DO YOU STILL *MISS* THEM?

Y-YOU...

NNRRK.

CAN'T... HANDLE THE *HEAT*... STONE?

I CAN HANDLE WHATEVER YOU *GOT*.

SHRKOOMM

DON'T MAKE ME GET *TOUGH.*

STAY THE HELL DOWN.

SKREEEEEEEEE

HE *WILL.*

EVERYONE SAW...

I ALREADY... *WON,* STONE.

I WON.

THANKS AGAIN, RAVEN.

YEAH. YOU'RE AS RIGHT AS RAIN, HUH?

NOT THAT I *REALLY* WAS WORRIED. A ROCKIN' GOOD TIME, WASN'T IT?

CHEERS TO THE TITANS.

I DON'T *DO* CHEERS. NOW I BETTER GET TO WORK. THERE ARE *OTHERS* THAT NEED MY HELP.

SHE'S *FREAKY.*

OH, *BE* NICE.

PRETTY AMAZING, VIC.

WHAT?

YOU TOOK LIGHT OUT ONE-ON-ONE.

EVERYONE ELSE *SOFTENED* HIM UP. HOW'RE THEY LOOKING?

GOOD. THOUGH STARFIRE AND NIGHTWING ARE ARGUING ON *WHO* INVITED DUELA DENT. THAT GIRL, THE "*JOKER'S DAUGHTER*" OR WHATEVER. SHE'S PRETTY *NUTS.*

SHE KEEPS GOING *ON* AND *ON* ABOUT HER DAYS WITH THE TITANS. I HEARD SHE WAS ON THE TEAM FOR, LIKE, *TWO* MINUTES.

MORE DELUDED THAN RAVAGER.

SO WHAT DO WE *DO* WITH HIM?

NIGHTWING CALLED SOMEONE FOR THE PICKUP.

WHO--?

US.

BATGIRL.

AND BATMAN.

I DIDN'T EVEN HEAR THE BATWING.

YOU'RE NOT SUPPOSED TO.

HEY, UH...Y'KNOW, YOU'RE ALWAYS WELCOME AT THE TOWER. BATGIRL...

BELLE REEVE'S READY.

GOTHAM NEEDS US.

HE'S ALWAYS *RUDE*, ISN'T HE? I MEAN, HE DIDN'T EVEN SAY *HI* TO ME.

YOU EXPECT HIM TO?

SOMETIMES I DON'T KNOW *HOW* ROBIN DEALS.

...I'M GOOD, THANKS. JUST NEED A CUP OF *COFFEE* TO WAKE UP.

VIC. LOOKS LIKE YOU NEED A PICK-ME-UP WORSE THAN *I*--

IS IT *TRUE*?

IS *WHAT* TRUE?

BEAST BOY USED TO BE ABLE TO TAKE DOWN LIGHT ON HIS OWN. *THIS* TIME IT TOOK *TWO DOZEN* TITANS.

LIGHT SAID THE LEAGUE TURNED HIM INTO AN *IDIOT*. THAT YOU LOBOTOMIZED HIM. IS IT *TRUE*?

DOES IT MATTER?

WHEN IT PUTS THE LIVES OF THESE KIDS IN DANGER YOU SURE AS HELL *BET* IT MATTERS.

YOU *KNOW* THAT, QUEEN.

YOU CREATED A *MONSTER*. A MONSTER *WE* HAVE TO WORRY ABOUT.

OLLIE!

YOU'RE *OKAY*.

YEAH, KID.

PERFECT.

EVERYTHING ALL RIGHT?

NOTHING WE CAN'T HANDLE.

GOOD, BECAUSE KORY, ROY AND I NEED TO LEAVE--

--SOMEONE JUST BROKE INTO OUTSIDERS HQ

DOCTOR LIGHT WASN'T LYING ABOUT THE JUSTICE LEAGUE.

SO THE LEAGUE DID IT? THEY CHANGED LIGHT'S MIND?

DID MY GRANDFATHER... WAS BARRY ALLEN A PART OF IT?

WONDER WOMAN--?

GREEN ARROW SAID SHE WASN'T THERE WHEN IT WENT DOWN. FLASH WAS.

WE'VE BEEN TOLD ALL OUR LIVES WE'RE SUPPOSED TO LOOK UP TO THE JUSTICE LEAGUE. THEY WERE ALWAYS THERE... LOOKING DOWN ON US...

SO WHO DO WE LOOK UP TO NOW?

EACH OTHER.

I DON'T THINK BATMAN WOULD DO THIS.

AND NEITHER WOULD SUPERMAN. NO WAY.

WE CAN'T JUST WRITE THEM OFF.

I DO NOT THINK THAT'S WHAT ANY OF US ARE FEELING, SUPERBOY.

THIS IS JUST AN ISSUE OF TRUST.

I DON'T KNOW WHAT'S GOING TO HAPPEN TO THE LEAGUE WITH THIS COMING OUT, AND IT WILL COME OUT--

--BUT, REGARDLESS, I DON'T WANT ANY SECRETS BETWEEN US.

I HAVE TO SAY SOMETHING.

I MEANT TO TELL YOU ALL... BEFORE THIS MESS WITH DOCTOR LIGHT. WHEN I *FIRST* GOT HERE I...

I RAN AWAY FROM HOME A FEW YEARS AGO. I SURVIVED ON THE STREETS. I MET *REAL* VILLAINS. GUYS LIKE DOCTOR LIGHT BUT WITHOUT THE CAPES AND THE POWERS.

I MADE MISTAKES. I WAS IN A BAD PLACE.

AND SOMEWHERE ALONG THE WAY...I...

I TESTED POSITIVE.

LIKE...?

YEAH.

I... I THOUGHT I WAS GOING TO HAVE NO PROBLEM TELLING YOU ALL THIS.

BUT I...I NEVER THOUGHT I'D ACTUALLY LIKE BEING HERE...

THAT I'D LIKE *YOU* ALL SO MUCH. ADMIRE...

I'VE KINDA GOT A SECRET TOO.

I DON'T MEAN TO BELITTLE WHAT YOU'RE GOING THROUGH BUT... I GOT SOMETHING IN *ME* LIKE YOU, MIA.

A BUNCH OF KIDS GOT *SICK* BECAUSE OF THE DISEASE THAT MADE ME INTO THIS MEAN, GREEN, ANIMAL MACHINE.

I DON'T KNOW *WHAT* IT'S GOING TO *DO* TO ME IN THE *FUTURE*, BUT AFTER SEEING "ANIMAL MAN"...I'M A LITTLE *SCARED*.

I STILL CAN'T STOP *FEEDING* OFF *EMOTIONS*. WHEN YOU ALL *SLEEP* HERE IN THE TOWER...

SOMETIMES YOUR *DREAMS*, BOTH *GOOD* AND *BAD*, BECOME MINE.

I'VE BEEN LIVING IN *DENIAL*.

I'VE SEEN *ARES* A LOT. WATCHING ME THROUGH WATER OR GLASS OR WHATEVER. IT *CREEPS* ME OUT.

HE GAVE ME MY *LASSO*, AND HE SAID HE WAS PREPARING ME FOR SOME KIND OF BIG *WAR*.

I'VE TRIED TO *THROW* THIS THING AWAY, BUT I *CAN'T*.

I GOTTA SECRET, *TOO*.

I RAN OUT OF CLEAN UNDERWEAR YESTERDAY SO I STOLE SOME OF BEAST BOY'S.

YOU *WHAT?*

AREN'T ANY OF YOU...WEIRDED OUT OR -- ?

UNCOMFORTABLE? SOME OF US, SURE.

BUT HOW *ELSE* DID YOU EXPECT US TO *REACT?* YOU THINK WE'RE GOING TO *KICK* YOU OUT?

WE WANT TO BE *SMART* ABOUT THIS. WE WANT TO TAKE ANY NECESSARY PRECAUTIONS TO KEEP YOU AND THE TITANS *SAFE.*

AND I'M SURE WE'LL HAVE QUESTIONS. MAYBE A *LOT* OF THEM.

I'LL ANSWER ANY YOU HAVE. IT WON'T BE EASY BUT...

WE KNOW WHAT IT'S LIKE TO BE DIFFERENT, MIA.

THAT'S *WHY* WE ALL COME TO THE TOWER.

AND ME AND VIC ARE HERE *SEVEN* DAYS A *WEEK.* YOU NEED ANYTHING, YOU JUST SWING BY.

LIKE ALL THOSE OTHER GUYS THAT SHOWED UP, YOU'RE A *TITAN,* SPEEDY! NOW AND FOREVER!

I'M A TITAN...?

I'M A TITAN.

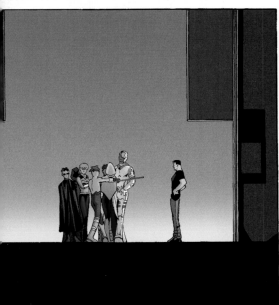

WHERE...?

WHERE ARE YOU *TAKING* ME?

YOU THINK I *LOST?* YOU THINK...

I THINK YOU NEED TO GO BACK TO *SLEEP,* DOC.

DID I DO WELL, DADDY?

YOU DID *PERFECT,* ROSE.

WHAT?

DEATHSTROKE?! WHAT IS THIS?

IT'S YOUR *LUCKY* DAY.

YOU'VE JUST BEEN *INVITED* INTO *HIGHER SOCIETY.*

END

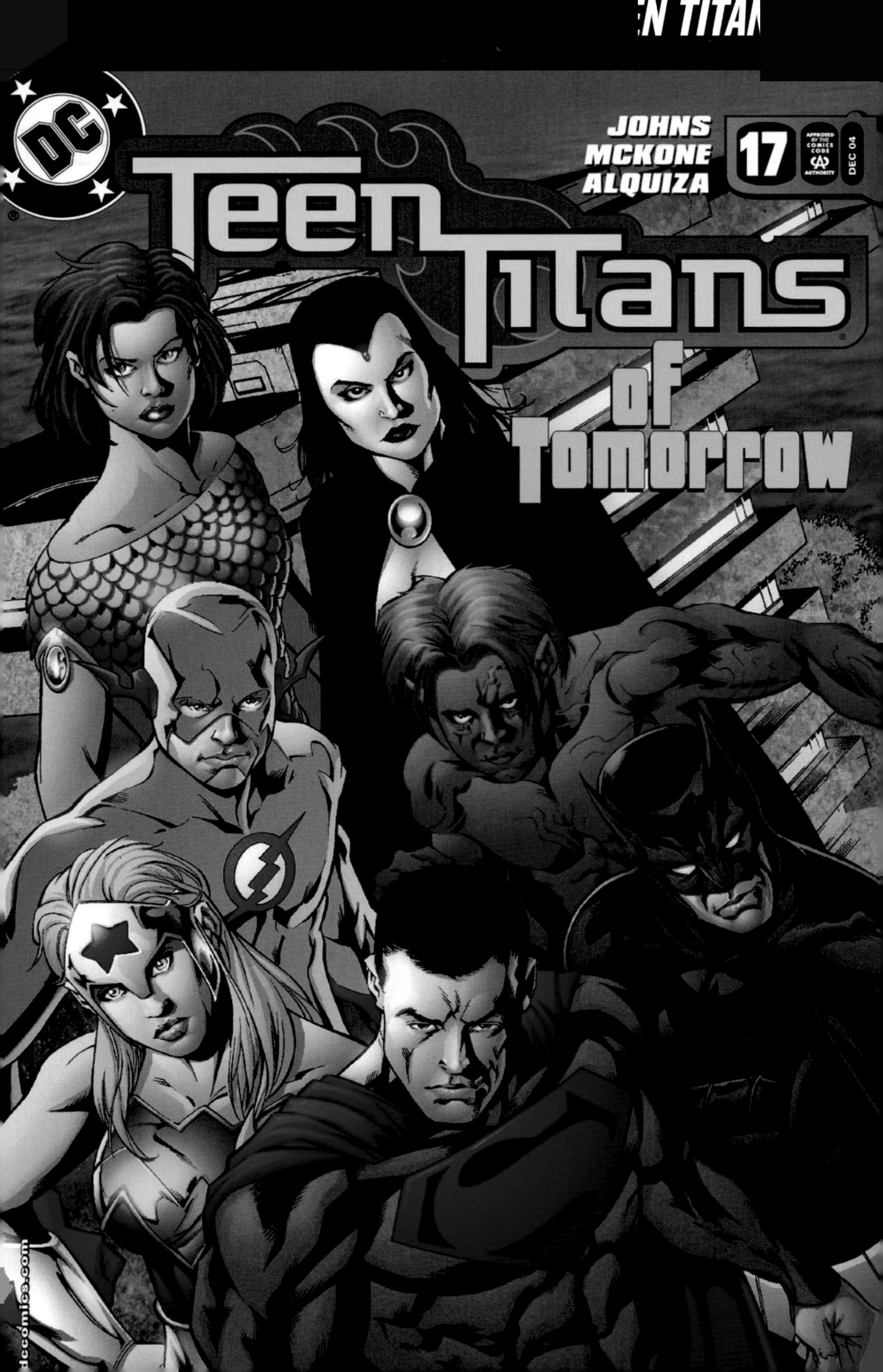
EN TITAN
DC
JOHNS
MCKONE
ALQUIZA
17
APPROVED BY THE COMICS CODE AUTHORITY
DEC 04
Teen Titans
of Tomorrow
dccomics.com

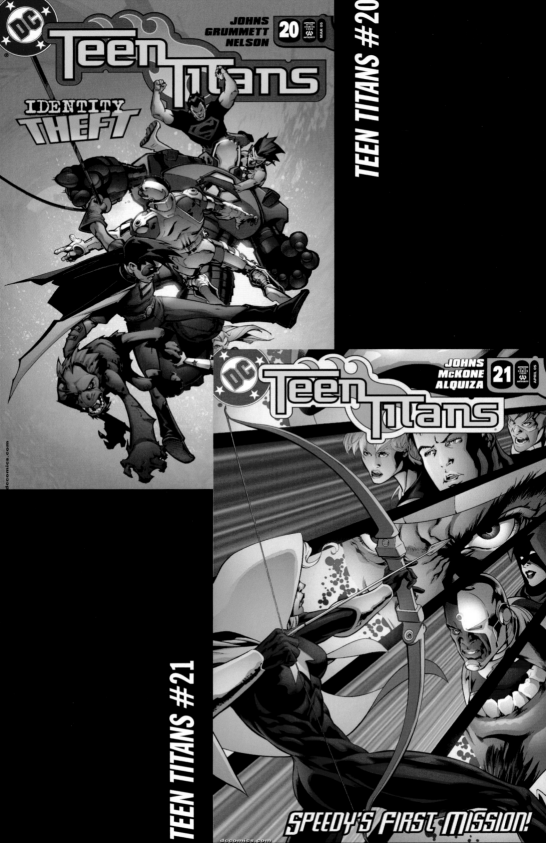

THE BRAVE AND THE BOLD #60

Following an initial team up in the pages of *The Brave and the Bold* #54 (July 1964), DC's teen sidekicks were brought back together a year later — this time billed officially as the Teen Titans and with Wonder Girl joining her male counterparts for the first time. The tale, written by DC mainstay Bob Haney and illustrated by Bruno Premiani, lay the groundwork for much of what was to follow.

T A third try-out secured the Teen Titans a regular title, launching with a February 1966 cover date. Initially scripted by Bob Haney, the book captured the cultural zeitgeist. Not only did it explore the so-called generation gap between young and old, it also highlighted political and social issues of particular concern to teenagers. Hot topics included racism, the environment and the peace movement.

T For a brief time, the Teen Titans even abandoned their costumed identities and behaved like Peace Corp activists, guiding fellow teenagers through the difficulties of everyday life. The original *Teen Titans* book was eventually cancelled, but was revived to even greater success in the 1980s as *The New Teen Titans*.

T The brainchild of writer Marv Wolfman and artist George Pérez, *The New Teen Titans* continued to explore generational themes, but focused squarely on the travails of the various team members. The Teen Titans went through typical teenage traumas, but their problems were amplified because of their super hero personas. The young heroes fell in and out of love and changed over time. As the Titans grew up, the audience grew up with them — making *The New Teen Titans* one of DC's best-selling titles.

APPROVED BY THE COMICS CODE AUTHORITY

JULY
NO 60

12¢

4 TEENAGE HEROES IN ONE BLAZING ADVENTURE!

ROBIN

WONDER GIRL

AQUALAD

KID FLASH

BUT AS THE HONDA "HORSES" MOVE TOWARD THE TOWN'S OUTSKIRTS...

THAT GIANT EYE -- WHERE'D IT COME FROM?

IT'S ANOTHER PART OF THE *SEPARATED MAN!* AND I'D BET MY LIFE IF YOU SAW ALL ITS FEATURES TOGETHER... THEY'D SPELL OUT THE FACE OF -- *PROFESSOR BRIAN HOLMES!*

THAT'S WHERE YOU'RE WRONG, MR. MAYOR! MY FACE IS RIGHT HERE WHERE IT BELONGS!

HOLMES! OFFICERS -- ARREST HIM! HE'S AN ESCAPED CONVICT!

BUT BEFORE THE POLICE CAN MOVE...

LOOK OUT! THE EYE'S DROPPING A *FLAMING TEAR* DOWN ON US!

GREAT JASPER! NOW THE *SEPARATED MAN* IS TRYING TO BURN DOWN THE TOWN!

THAT'S BECAUSE HE'S AFTER SOMETHING WHICH ONLY *I* CAN LOCATE! GET BACK -- THE FAHRENHEIT'S TERRIFIC!

AT THAT INSTANT...

KID FLASH!

DON'T WORRY... I'LL COOL OFF THOSE HOT TEAR DROPS!

12

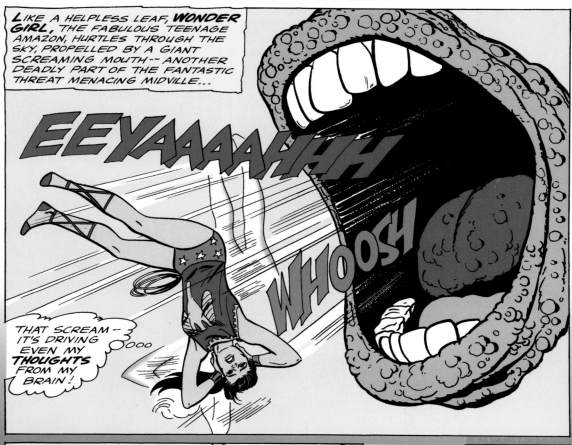

LIKE A HELPLESS LEAF, **WONDER GIRL**, THE FABULOUS TEENAGE AMAZON, HURTLES THROUGH THE SKY, PROPELLED BY A GIANT SCREAMING MOUTH -- ANOTHER DEADLY PART OF THE FANTASTIC THREAT MENACING MIDVILLE...

EEYAAAAHHH

WHOOSH

THAT SCREAM -- IT'S DRIVING EVEN MY **THOUGHTS** FROM MY BRAIN!

FIGHTING DESPERATELY TO KEEP CONTROL OF HER THOUGHTS, THE TUMBLING TEENAGER BEGINS COUNTING...

ONE-TWO-THREE... I THINK THAT I SHALL NEVER SEE -- A BILLBOARD LOVELY AS A TREE...

BILLBOARD! THAT'S IT--!

EEYAAAAAHH

WHOOSH

WHOOOSH

TRUCK

17

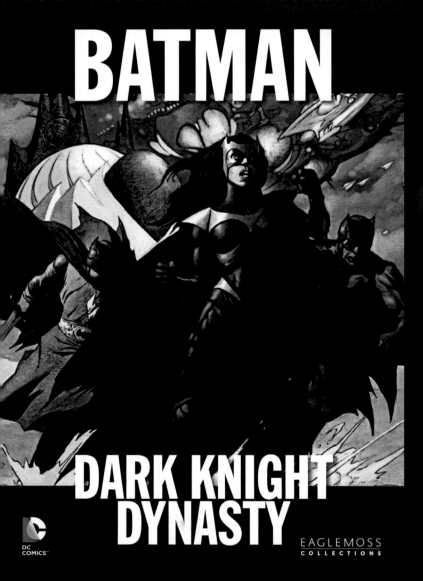

VOLUME 76

s the new Flash, Bart Allen, tries to strip himself of his speed powers, hi
est friend Griffin Gray struggles with abilities that cause him to age rapi

DC COMICS GRAPHIC NOVEL COLLECTION

THE FLASH

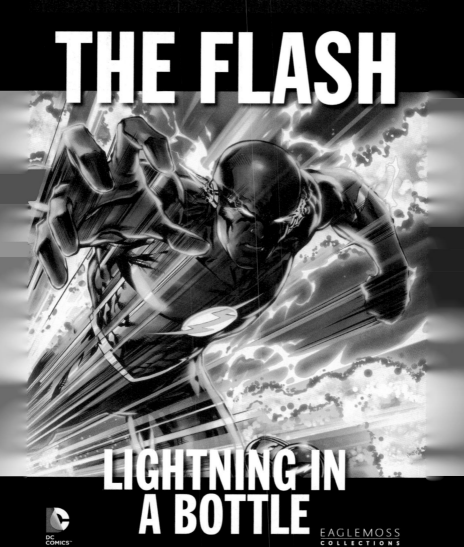

LIGHTNING IN
A BOTTLE

EAGLEMOSS
COLLECTIONS

DC
COMICS™

PLUS BART ALLEN AS IMPULSE IN *IMPULSE #1*

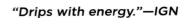

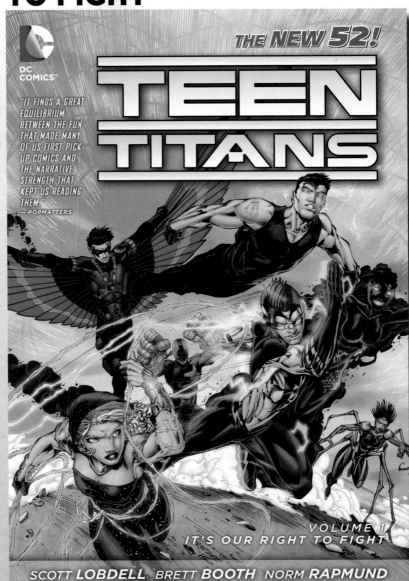